Master of Disguises

Master of Disguises

CHARLES SIMIC

HOUGHTON MIFFLIN HARCOURT
2010 BOSTON   NEW YORK

For information about permission to reproduce selections from this book, write to Permissions, Houghton Mifflin Harcourt Publishing Company, 215 Park Avenue South, New York, New York 10003.

www.hmhbooks.com

Library of Congress Cataloging-in-Publication Data
Simic, Charles, date.
Master of disguises : poems / Charles Simic.
p. cm.
ISBN 978-0-547-39709-2
I. Title.
PS3569.I4725M37 2010
811'.54—dc22   2009047470

Book design by Brian Moore

Printed in the United States of America

DOC 10 9 8 7 6 5 4 3 2

Some of these poems have previously appeared in the following magazines to whose editors grateful acknowledgment is made: *The New Yorker, Notre Dame Review, Margie, London Review of Books, New York Review of Books, Southern Review, Virginia Quarterly Review, Poetry, Five Points, Boulevard, Times Literary Supplement, Daedalus, New Welsh Review, Paris Review, Tuesday Magazine, Tin House,* and *Salmagundi.* The poem "Carrying On Like a Crow" appeared in *The Best American Poetry 2010.*

for Helen

Everything as unreal as real can be.

— WALLACE STEVENS

Contents

I

The Invisible One

You read today about a child
Kept for years in a closet
By his crazy parents
On a street you walked often.

Busy with your own troubles,
You saw little, heard nothing
Of what was said around you,
As you made your way home

Past loving young couples
Carrying flowers and groceries,
Pushing baby carriages,
Hanging back to scold a dog.

Master of Disguises

Surely, he walks among us unrecognized:
Some barber, store clerk, delivery man,
Pharmacist, hairdresser, bodybuilder,
Exotic dancer, gem cutter, dog walker,
The blind beggar singing, O Lord, remember me,

Some window decorator starting a fake fire
In a fake fireplace while mother and father watch
From the couch with their frozen smiles
As the street empties and the time comes
For the undertaker and the last waiter to head home.

O homeless old man, standing in a doorway
With your face half hidden,
I wouldn't even rule out the black cat crossing the street,
The bare light bulb swinging on a wire
In a subway tunnel as the train comes to a stop.

Nineteen Thirty-eight

That was the year the Nazis marched into Vienna,
Superman made his debut in Action Comics,
Stalin was killing off his fellow revolutionaries,
The first Dairy Queen opened in Kankakee, Ill.,
As I lay in my crib peeing in my diapers.

"You must've been a beautiful baby," Bing Crosby sang.
A pilot the newspapers called Wrong Way Corrigan
Took off from New York heading for California
And landed instead in Ireland, as I watched my mother
Take a breast out of her blue robe and come closer.

There was a hurricane that September causing a movie
       theater
At Westhampton Beach to be lifted out to sea.
People worried the world was about to end.
A fish believed to have been extinct for seventy million years
Came up in a fishing net off the coast of South Africa.

I lay in my crib as the days got shorter and colder,
And the first heavy snow fell in the night
Making everything very quiet in my room.
I thought I heard myself cry for a long, long time.

Scenes of the Old Life

Washing hung from the fire escapes.
Boys threw cats from rooftops.
War veterans hopped on crutches,
Pitching pennies and smoking reefers.

Writers destined to remain obscure
Wrote late into the night
Using a pencil and the kind of notebook
Their children took to school in the morning.

Outside a club advertising exotic dancing girls,
A man in a crumpled white suit
Staggered with a knife in his heart,
One dark eyebrow raised in surprise.

In winter, rain fell as if it meant to fall forever.
We kept the gas oven lit to warm ourselves,
While mother cried and cried chopping onions
And my one goldfish swam in a pickle jar.

The Elusive Something

Was it in the smell of freshly baked bread
That came out to meet me in the street?
The face of a girl carrying a white dress
From the cleaners with her eyes half closed?

The sight of a building blackened by fire
Where once I went to look for work?
The toothless old man passing out leaflets
For a clothing store going out of business?

Or was it the woman pushing a baby carriage
About to turn the corner? I ran after,
As if the little one lying in it was known to me,
And found myself alone on a busy street

I didn't recognize, feeling like someone
Out for the first time after a long illness,
Who sees the world with his heart,
Then hurries home to forget how it felt.

Blind Man Feeding Pigeons

Where did he get all these crumbs?
He tosses right and left
As the birds flock to him,
One alighting on his shoulder.

A few days later I had my answer
In a bakery where he turned up
To collect stale rolls,
Thanking one and all.

Then last night I thought of him
Sitting on a narrow bed
Breaking bread with his hands,
Unless, of course, he was dead.

Preachers Warn

This peaceful world of ours is ready for destruction—
And still the sun shines, the sparrows come
Each morning to the bakery for crumbs.
Next door, two men deliver a bed for a pair of newlyweds
And stop to admire a bicycle chained to a parking meter.
Its owner is making lunch for his ailing grandmother.
He heats the soup and serves it to her in a bowl.

The windows are open, there's a warm breeze.
The young trees on our street are delirious to have leaves.
Italian opera is on the radio, the volume too high.
Brevi e tristi giorni visse, a baritone sings.
Everyone up and down our block can hear him.
Something about the days that remain for us to enjoy
Being few and sad. Not today, Maestro Verdi!

At the hairdresser's a girl leaps out of a chair,
Her blond hair bouncing off her bare shoulders
As she runs out the door in her high heels.
"I must be off," says the handsome boy to his grandmother.
His bicycle is where he left it.
He rides it casually through the heavy traffic
His white shirttails fluttering behind him
Long after everyone else has come to a sudden stop.

Worriers Anonymous

We are a doomsday sect
With a membership that runs into millions.
The waitress stepping out for a quick smoke
And the yellow dog tied outside the bank,
We don't need nametags to know each other.

Inmates of invisible prisons, hospitals and madhouses,
It's the season of vague premonitions,
Rambling thoughts, deepening panic.
Yesterday, some lucky fellow won the lottery,
An old lady got killed by a falling brick.

It's the way the old couple hold hands—
They may have just come out of an elevator
That had been stuck for hours,
Grateful for a breather before some fresh worry
Draws close to darken their day.

Scribbled in the Dark

A shout in the street.
Someone locking horns with his demon.
Then, calm returning.
The wind tousling the leaves.
The birds in their nests
Pleased to be rocked back to sleep.
Night turning cool.
Streams of blood in the gutter
Waiting for sunrise.

Old Man

Backed myself into a dark corner one day,
Found a boy there
Forgotten by teachers and classmates,
His shoulders slumped,
The hair on his head already gray.
Friend, I said.

While you stood here staring at the wall,
They shot a president,
Some guy walked on the moon,
Dolly, the girl we all loved,
Took too many sleeping pills and died
In a hotel room in Santa Monica.

Now and then I thought of you,
Listening to the squeak of the chalk
On the blackboard,
The sighs and whispers
Of unknown children
Bent over their lessons,
The mice running in the night.

Visions of unspeakable loveliness
Must've come to you in your misery:
Cloudless skies on long June evenings,
Trees full of cherries in our orchard,
To make you ache and want to be with me,
Driving a cab in New York City.

Among the Exiles

One met former cabinet ministers,
University professors, defrocked priests and officers,
Feeding pigeons from a park bench,
Squinting into foreign newspapers
And telling anyone who happened to ask
Not to bother their heads about the truth.

On the use of murder to improve the world
They had many vivid memories
As they huddled in their dim kitchens,
Clipping supermarket coupons,
Shifting the loose dentures in their mouths
While waiting for the teakettle to boil.

They ate in restaurants with waiters older than themselves,
Musicians whose fingers bled
As they picked at their instruments
Making some tipsy widow burst into sobs
On hearing a tune her husband the general loved,
The one who sent thousands to their deaths.

Wildflowers

There were wildflowers along the road to hell.
The wind blew and the flowers
Danced in the ditches, alone or in pairs,
In that cheerful way flowers have.
You had to be there to see them
And the guard towers coming into view.

I wasn't. Still, one hot summer afternoon
As I lay resting, their bright colors came to me,
And that dusty road and that long ditch
Where the wind played with them
Carrying their scent past the barbed wire,
Or so I thought, too scared to imagine the rest.

Dogs Pity Their Masters

They sit at their feet after the dinner is over
And watch their expressions darken
As they read the papers or listen to their wives
Speak of troubles greater than their own,

After which, only the silence of the peaceful countryside
Can be heard; the trees full of leaves
Busy with their own worries; the one lit lamp
Not strong enough to keep the shadows at bay.

Nancy Jane

Grandma laughing on her deathbed.
Eternity, the quiet one, listening in.

Like moths around an oil lamp we were.
Like rag dolls tucked away in the attic.

In walked a cat with a mouthful of feathers.
(How about that?)

A dark little country store full of gravediggers'
    children buying candy.
(That's how we looked that night.)

The young man pumping gas spoke of his friends:
    the clouds.
It was such a sad story, it made everyone laugh.

A bird called out of a tree, but received no answer.

The beauty of that last moment
Like a red sail on the bay at sunset,

Or like a wheel breaking off a car
And roaming the world on its own.

At Adam and Evie Tanning Salon

It may be night; it may be drizzling a bit,
The streets all puddled and dark,
The ghostly storefronts awaiting their wrecking ball,
The one grocery store still in business
Being robbed at gunpoint by two punks,

As Evie rubs scented oil on your chest,
The sea sparkles on the overhead screen,
Adam mixes cocktails in the cabana,
And the rows of palm trees sway along in the wind
In that slow, dignified way they have.

I'm telling you, that place is heaven!
The courthouse clock striking two,
The cops nodding off in their cruiser,
The steady rain changing over to snow,
While you lie in the sand working on your tan.

Dark Is the Night

Crumpled under a doomsday sign,
You roamed the streets
Convinced the day will come
You'll be meeting the Lord,
His face coming briefly into view
As the crowd pushes and parts open
At the subway entrance.

Come night, you vanished
With your soiled white raincoat,
Your gray beard and flowing hair
And your homemade sign
Warning of God's displeasure.

One time, with nothing better to do,
I followed your usual route,
Peeking into doorways and alleyways
Favored by the old and the destitute,
Wondering if you had a friend,
Or were you all alone in the world?

II

Old Soldier

By the time I was five,
I had fought in hundreds of battles,
Had killed thousands
And suffered many wounds
Only to rise and fight again.

After the bombing raid, the sky was full
Of flying cinders and birds.
My mother took me by the hand
And led me into the garden
Where the cherry trees were in flower.

There was a cat grooming herself
Whose tail I wanted to pull,
But I let her be for a moment,
Since I was busy swinging at flies
With a sword made of cardboard.

All I needed was a horse to ride,
Like the one hitched to a hearse,
Outside a pile of rubble,
Waiting with its head lowered
For them to finish loading the coffins.

Carrying On Like a Crow

Are you authorized to speak
For these trees without leaves?
Are you able to explain
What the wind intends to do
With a man's shirt and a woman's nightgown
Left on the laundry line?
What do you know about dark clouds?
Ponds full of fallen leaves?
Old-model cars rusting in a driveway?
Who gave you the permission
To look at the beer can in a ditch?
The white cross by the side of the road?
The swing set in the widow's yard?
Ask yourself, if words are enough,
Or if you'd be better off
Flapping your wings from tree to tree
And carrying on like a crow.

The Absent One

Someone's late coming home.
The lamp left for him in the window
Burns as the day breaks,
And will burn for months after.

Our small street is dark at night.
The birdcages are covered early.
The goldfish barely stir in their jars.
Even the porch lights are off,

Leaving only his window lit
For moths to pay their respects
Until the weather turns cold
And the roofs are white with snow.

Driving Home

Minister of our coming doom, preaching
On the car radio, how right
Your hell and damnation sound to me
As I travel these small, bleak roads
Thinking of the mailman's son
The Army sent back in a sealed coffin.

His house is around the next turn.
A forlorn mutt sits in the yard
Waiting for someone to come home.
I can see the TV is on in the living room,
Canned laughter in the empty house
Like the sound of beer cans tied to a hearse.

The Sparrow

Regarding the current wars,
I heard them say on TV
That they will last forever
Since our enemies are many.

There'll be plenty of business
For those making bombs,
Uniforms and hospital beds,
And, of course, coffins.

Sparrow, hopping in the yard,
If our president is right,
You and I may be on crutches
Next time you pay us a visit.

Same-as-Ever

There was a stonemason's yard,
But its dozen gravestones
Had no names on them yet.
Otherwise, not much to see here.

Early evening, the small stores
On Main Street already closed.
A few porch lights here and there.
The silence of bowed heads
Saying grace and gritting their teeth.

Nothing ever happens here,
Except for these foreign wars
That maim the young boys
And leave their golden girls
To hustle drinks in local dives.

Father in Heaven

I had not thought there were so many
Whose sole delight in life
Was to bring misery to others.
How the crowds adore them!
How they cheer their endless wars!
It makes me lose my faith.

Braving this January wind and snow,
After a night of bad dreams
And spells of anger at him
For dying young and leaving me here
To beat with raw fists
Against the padlocked cemetery gate,
Begging man or god to let me in.

Sightseeing in the Capital

These grand old buildings
With their spacious conference rooms,
Leather-padded doors,
Where they weigh life and death
Without a moment of fear
Of ever being held accountable,

And then withdraw to dine in style
And drink to each other's health
In private clubs and country estates,
While we linger on the sidewalk
Admiring the rows of windows
The evening sun has struck blind.

Daughters of Memory

There were three of them, always three,
Sunbathing side by side on the beach,
The sound of waves and children's voices so soothing
It was hard to stay awake.

When I woke, the sun was setting.
The three friends knelt in a circle
Taking turns to peek into a small mirror
And comb their hair with the same comb.

Months later, I happened to see two of them
Running in the rain after school,
Ducking into a doorway with a pack of cigarettes
And a glance at me in my new uniform.

In the end, there was just one girl left,
Tall and beautiful,
Making late rounds in a hospital ward,
Past a row of beds, one of which was mine.

Private Miseries

More than this crippled veteran playing the banjo,
I have no right to grumble,
More than this old woman cracking open her purse
To give him a quarter,

Lest they both take offense and beat me
On the head with one of his crutches.
My own anguish must remain unspoken,
Hidden behind a firm stride and a smile.

One day I knelt down and cursed God
For all the suffering and injustice he consents to.
Since then, I have felt even more alone.
Like a lifelong widower forever unconsoled

I pass the homeless huddled in doorways
Upon a winter morning and dare not
Grouse about my own sleepless night,
And my cold feet that make me hurry past them.

The End of a Parade

The quickly dispersing few
Who'd seen it pass down the avenue
Were not able to tell me
What was being commemorated.

Rows of unsmiling children
Dressed in black went by listlessly
Carrying small American flags.
Then came men slumped in wheelchairs,
Followed by others on crutches.

There was a marching band, too,
That never played a note
And an old Italian selling ices
Who shrugged his shoulders
When I asked him who they were.

Our Salvation

What I hate are short winter days,
Cold and snowless afternoons,
The dark night in a hurry to fall
After the last school bus passes.

I dislike a woman who won't light
But one lamp in the house,
Who keeps the heat way down
And wears three sweaters and a shawl.

What drives me to despair are meals
Eaten in silence with the TV on,
The recital of the day's horrors
Followed by a grim weather report.

It breaks my heart to go to bed
Every night in a room without heat
With the one who still has strength
To pray to God for our salvation.

Solitude

The only home you and I ever had.
No bigger than a matchbox—
Or else as vast as the sky full of stars—
With you as the sole tenant
Grateful for a flea bite to scratch
As you sit recalling the night
Someone knocked on your door.

You were afraid to open, but when you did,
There she was asking to borrow a candle.
You told her you didn't have one.
The two of you stood face to face
Between two dark apartments
Unable to think of anything else to say
Before turning your backs on each other.

In That Big House

When she still knew how to make shadows speak
By sitting with them a long time,
They talked about her handsome father,
His long absence, and how the quiet
Would fill the house on snowy evenings.

"Tell us, child, are you afraid?" they'd ask,
While the girl listened for steps in the hallway,
The long, dim one with a full-length mirror
That's been going blind like her grandmother
Who could no longer find or thread a needle

As she sat in the parlor remembering some actors
Her son brought to dinner one night,
The one young woman who wandered off by herself
And was found later, after a long search,
Floating naked in the black water of the pond.

Puppet Maker

In his fear of solitude, he made us.
Fearing eternity, he gave us time.
I hear his white cane thumping
Up and down the hall.

I expect neighbors to complain, but no.
The little girl who sobbed
When her daddy crawled into her bed
Is quiet now.

It's quarter to two.
On this street of darkened pawnshops,
Welfare hotels and tenements,
One or two ragged puppets are awake.

Sad as a Ship in a Bottle

Sad as a matchbox in a house
Where they've stopped smoking.
Sad as a soap of a movie queen
After she steps out of the shower.
Sad as the love pill
In a pocket of a dead man.
Happy as a mouse in a rocking chair.
Happy as a pair of dentures . . .
No, wait a minute! Something's wrong here!
Sad as a maybug in June.
Sad as a hotdog-eating champion
Having dinner in a fish restaurant.

Graveside Oration

Our late friend hated blue skies,
Bible-quoting preachers,
Politicians kissing babies,
Women who are all sweetness.

He liked drunks in church,
Nudists playing volleyball,
Stray dogs making friends,
Birds singing of fair weather as they crap.

III

Streets Paved with Gold

A row of palatial madhouses,
Each with a well-tended lawn,
A sprinkler and a barbecue pit
Smoking in the backyard,

And someone in a tree swing
After the sun has gone down,
Too old to be swinging
And to be wearing no clothes,

Blowing random notes on a toy trumpet
At the converging darkness,
And the one little white cloud
Dilly-dallying in the evening sky.

Darkened Chessboard

With the night already fallen,
It's hard to see who is playing,
Who is watching the game
At the little table in the park
Where no one says a word,
Engrossed as they are in the next move.

Their dinners are getting cold.
The wives they left behind
Are worrying themselves sick
While they dither here
On the lookout for the white queen
Last seen snatching a black pawn.

Double Feature

The lit marquee of a movie theater
At the end of a dark small-town street.
The one in the ticket booth interrupting her knitting
To look over her wire-rim glasses
Whether anyone's coming to see the show.

Where's the pretty girl who cried every time?
The math teacher and his blind old mother?
The swarms of kids who sat in the first row?
The tough barmaid on her night off?
The undertaker who'd fall asleep and snore?

Late August night of another century.
The soundtrack now and then loud enough
To hear the pistol shots on the sidewalk,
But not the sighs of lovers on the screen,
Holding hands and getting ready to say goodbye.

The Boardwalks Are Deserted

Duck in a shooting gallery, it's Sunday.
Your tormentors have now dispersed
To nurse their hangovers in private,
Or to stand with heads bowed in church.

Where is the couple who shared
A slice of pizza between kisses?
A man on all fours chasing a dog?
The old lady tipping her toe in the sea?

Even the fortuneteller's shack is closed.
The cards warning of dark strangers,
Loves to be sundered, hopes wrecked,
Lie on her table with their faces down.

End-of-the-season chill already in the air.
The gulls have the spilled contents
Of a trash basket to keep them happy,
And I have my little ducky to think about.

Little Boat, Take Care

We see nothing except what is unimportant to see,
I recall my father saying.
His room was empty of furniture.
Even the wall next to his bed where he rested his head
Now seemed unfamiliar.

Come evening, store windows have their own reveries.
When found out, they appear surprised
To see us and not someone else walking by.
Lost soul, where have you been hiding?
I thought I heard one of them whisper

As I made my way back to the car
Which sat alone in a huge parking lot
With a pretty view of the bridge and the bay.
One little sailboat still left on it,
Heading bravely out to the open sea.

Dead Season

This landscape with its somber skies
Must have fallen in love
With a story by Edgar Allan Poe.
One of its birch trees could be his Eleanora,
And the other, farther on, Ligeia.

Life is a dream within a dream,
Whisper the fallen leaves under our feet.
The old house, softly lit from within
By its copper pots and mirrors,
Seems even more abandoned this evening.

What if I were to knock on its door?
Keeping in mind, as I push it open
And enter cautiously, that for Poe
Beauty could be the cause of sudden death.

Summer Storm

I'm going over to see what those weeds
By the stone wall are fretting about.
Perhaps they don't care for the way
The shadows creep across the lawn
In the silence of the afternoon.

The sky keeps being blue,
Though we hear no birds,
See no butterflies among the flowers,
No ants running over our feet.
As for the trees in our yard,

They bend their branches ever so slightly
In deference to something
About to make its entrance
Of which we know nothing,
Spellbound as we are by the deepening quiet.

The Melon

There was a melon fresh from the garden
So ripe the knife slurped
As it cut it into six slices.
The children were going back to school.
Their mother, passing out paper plates,
Would not live to see the leaves fall.

I remember a hornet, too, that flew in
Through the open window
Mad to taste the sweet fruit
While we ducked and screamed,
Covered our heads and faces,
And sat laughing after it was gone.

The Lovers

In the woods one fair Sunday,
When we were children,
We came upon a couple lying on the ground.

Hand in hand, ourselves afraid
Of losing our way, we saw
What we first thought was a patch of snow,

The two clutching each other naked
On the bare ground, the wind
Swaying the branches over them

As we stole by, never to find out
Who they were, never to mention it afterwards
To each other, or to anyone else.

Bright and Early

Out of a bad dream's
Smoldering ruins,
A flight of crows'
Bloodied and dripping wings

Soared high over me
This morning
Like flying scissors
Snipping at threads,

Making my puppet head
Jerk sideways,
My feet jitterbug
On the patch of ice in the yard.

The Empress

My beloved, you who spend your nights
Torturing me
By holding up one mirror after another
To me in the dark,
If there's anything I know to say or do today,
I merit no praise for it,
But owe it to the subtlety of your torments,
And your perseverance in keeping me awake.

All the same, who gave you the right
To judge me in my wretchedness?
What soul white as snow
Compiled this endless list of misdeeds
You read to me every night?
The airs you put on when I tell you to stop
Would make one believe
You were once a bedmate of a Chinese emperor.

I like it best when we do not say a word.
When we lie side by side
Like two lovers after their passion is spent.
Once again, day is breaking.
A small bird in the trees is pouring her heart out
At the miracle of the coming light.
It hurts.
The beauty of a night spent sleepless.

In My Long Night

I have toiled like a spider at his web
In the dome of a church
Where only the upraised eyes of martyrs
In their torments could see me.

Where one cold spring day,
With rumors of war in the air,
My young parents brought me
To be baptized by the priest.

Where years after, my grandmother
Was to lie in an open coffin
Looking pleased to be done with
Having to bury other people.

Where I once saw a crow walk in,
Lured by the gold on the altar
And the light the candles cast,
While I dangled up there by a thread.

Trees in the Yard

Quick-tempered tribe, this is your season,
You who take scant notice of a breeze in winter
And will forbear a major snowstorm,
Now take offense at any little puff of wind,
And get-to-whispering and gossip-mongering.

What calumnies are you exchanging at night?
You who are usually so discreet and wise.
How am I to comprehend these sudden outbursts,
These long lists of concocted grievances
You dwell on and take so much to heart?

To us, who are already awake and distressed
Regarding some other matter, you appear to
Show maternal understanding one moment, and scorn
The next, until driven out of our wits
We sit up in bed and turn on the lights.

The Toad

It'll be a while before my friends
See me in the city,
A while before we roam the streets
Late at night
Shouting each other's names
To point out some sight too wonderful
Or too terrifying
To give it a name in a hurry.

I'm staying put in the country,
Rising early,
Listening to the birds
Greet the light,
And when they fall quiet,
To the wind in the leaves
Which are as numerous here
As the crowds in your city.

God never made a day as beautiful as today,
A neighbor was saying.
I sat in the shade after she left
Mulling that one over,
When a toad hopped out of the grass
And, finding me harmless,
Hopped over my foot on his way to the pond.

Summer Light

It likes empty churches
At the blue hour of dawn.

The shadows parting
Like curtains in a sideshow,

The eyes of the crucified
Staring down from the cross

As if seeing his bloody feet
For the very first time.

The Tree No One Visits

So I did. I climbed one afternoon
Up that steep, rocky hill,
Stopping to rest and admire a wildflower
And the view of the lake
In the valley down below.

I would have liked a goat for company.
A black-and-white one with a bell
To go ahead, graze awhile and break
The quiet as he resumes his ascent
To where a tree stands dark and silent

Waiting all these years for someone
To sit in its shade at ease with himself.
Even the wind that's always thinking up
Little games for its leaves to play,
In no hurry now to disturb the peace.

Keep This to Yourself

There are country roads now that are empty.
They'll hold on to the light of the day
A bit longer, mindful some boy
May be heading home after a game.

Whoever he is, he'll have to hurry.
This lovely moment won't last long.
The road before him lies white
Here and there under the dark trees,

As if some mad girl in the neighborhood
Had emptied her linen closet
And had been spreading her things
Over the soft late-summer dust.

IV

The Invisible

1

It was always here.
Its vast terrors concealed
By this costume party
Of flowers and birds
And children playing in the garden.

Only the leaves tell the truth.
They rustle darkly,
Then fall silent as if listening
To a dragonfly
Who may know a lot more of the invisible,

Or why else would its wings be
So translucent in the light,
So swift to take flight,
One barely notices
It's been here and gone.

2

Don't the shadows know something about it?
The way they, too, come and go
As if paying a visit to that other world
Where they do what they do
Before hurrying back to us.

Just today I was admiring the one I cast
As I walked alone in the street
And was about to engage it in conversation
On this very topic
When it took leave of me suddenly.

Shadow, I said, what message
Will you bring back to me,
And will it be full of dark ambiguities
I can't even begin to imagine
As I make my slow way in the midday sun?

3

It may be hiding behind a door
In some office building,
Where one day you found yourself
After hours
With no one to ask for directions,
Among the hundreds of doors
All lacking information what sort of business,
What sort of drudgery goes on
Inside its narrow, poorly lit rooms.

Some detective agency
That'll find God for a small fee?
Some company ready to insure you,
Should one day,
Despite the promises of your parish priest,
You turn up in hell?

The long hallway ends at a window
Where even the light of the dying day
Seems old and dusty.
It understands what waiting is,
And when found out
Appears surprised to see you here.

4

The moment you shut off the lamp,
Here they are again,
The two dead people
You called your parents.

You'd hoped you'd see tonight
The girl you loved once,
And that other one who let you
Slip a hand under her skirt.

Instead, here's that key in a saucer of small change
That wouldn't open any lock,
The used condom you found in church,
The lame crow your neighbor kept.

Here's the fly you once tortured,
A rock you threw at your best friend,
The pig that let out a scream
As the knife touched its throat.

5

People here still tell stories
About a blind old man
Who rolled dice on the sidewalk
And paid children
In the neighborhood
To tell him what number came up.

When they were away in school,
He'd ask anyone
Whose steps he heard,
The mailman making his rounds,
The undertakers loading a coffin in their black wagon,
And you, too, mister,
Should you happen to come along.

6

Dark evening, gray old tenement,
A white cat in one window,
An old man eating his dinner in another.
Everyone else hidden from view,

Like the one who waits for the tub
To fill up with hot water
While she undresses before a mirror
Already beginning to steam over.

Imagination, devil's helper,
Made me glimpse her two breasts
As I hurried by with my face tucked in my collar,
Because the wind was raw.

7

Dear Miss Russell:

Nights, you took me on a private tour
Of the empty town library.
I could hardly keep up
As you darted along the rows of books,
Whispering their names,
Pointing out the ones I ought to read,

Then forgetting all about me,
Pulling the light cord
And leaving me in the dark
To grope for a book
Among the shelves,
Surely the wrong one,

As I was soon to learn
At the checkout desk
Under your pitying gaze
That followed me into the street
Where I dared not stop
To see what I held in my hand
Until I had rounded the corner.

8

A rusty key from a cigar box full of keys
In a roadside junk shop.
The one I held on to a long time
Before I let it slip
Through my fingers.

Most likely, when it was still in use,
The reclusive author
Of "The Minister's Black Veil"
Was still cooped up
In his mother's house in Salem.

It opened a small drawer
With a stack of yellowed letters
In a dresser with a mirror
That gave back a pale face
With a pair of feverish eyes

In a room with a view
Of black, leafless trees
And red clouds hurrying at sunset,
Where soon tears fell
Causing the key to go rusty.

9

O Persephone, is it true what they say,
That everything that is beautiful,
Even for one fleeting moment,
Descends to you, never to return?

Dressmaker pinning a red dress in a store
     window,
Old man walking your sickly old dog,
Even you little children holding hands
As you cross the busy street with your
     teacher,

What hope do you have for us today?
With the sky darkening so early,
The first arriving flakes of snow,
Falling here and there, then everywhere.

10

Invisible one, watching the snow
Through a dark window
From a row of dark schoolhouse windows,
Making sure the snowflakes fall
In proper order
Where they were fated to fall
In the gray yard,
And hush the moment they do.

The crow nodding his head
As he walks by
Must've been a professor of philosophy
In a previous life
Who despite changed circumstances
Still opens his beak
From time to time
As if to address his adoring students,
And seeing nothing but snow,
Looks up puzzled
At one of the dark windows.

11

Bird comforting the afflicted
With your song,
The one or two lying awake
In the vast slumber
Of small town and countryside,

Who know nothing of each other
As they listen intently
To every little tweet
Afraid they'll do something
To make it hush.

In the cool, silvery light,
The outline of the window visible,
Some trees in the yard
About to let go of the night,
The others in no big hurry.

V

And Who Are You, Sir?

I'm just a shuffling old man,
Ventriloquizing
For a god
Who hasn't spoken to me once.

The one with the eyes of a goat
Grazing alone
On some high mountain meadow
In the long summer dusk.